The Catholic Church and the race question

by the Reverend Father YVES M.-J. CONGAR, O.P.

THE RACE QUESTION AND MODERN THOUGHT

THE
CATHOLIC CHURCH
AND THE
RACE QUESTION.

by

The Reverend Father YVES M.-J. CONGAR, O.P.

UNESCO

Published by the United Nations
Educational, Scientific and Cultural Organization
Place de Fontenoy, Paris-7^e
1st impression November 1953
2nd impression March 1961
3rd impression September 1966
Printed by Imprimerie Offset-Aubin, Poitiers

*The pamphlets so far published by Unesco in the series
"The Race Question in Modern Science" have been
designed to provide a succinct survey of the present state
of the race question as it appears to anthropologists,
geneticists and sociologists.*

*But the problems raised by prejudice and racial dis-
crimination have not merely a scientific bearing. It would
be naïvely optimistic to think that racial conflicts could
be solved, and the tragedies they cause ended, simply
by bringing the findings of modern scientists to the
knowledge of the public. The race question also affects
man's conscience; and religions and philosophies have
long concerned themselves with it and taken one stand
or another with regard to it.*

*The time is therefore ripe to state the attitude of the
world's main religions and philosophical systems towards
the diversity of human types.*

*The first pamphlet in this new series "The Race
Question and Modern Thought" is written by the
Reverend Father Congar, of the Dominican Order, whose
manuscript has received the imprimatur of the ecclesiastical authorities.*

INTRODUCTION

Readers of previous pamphlets on *"The Race Question in Modern Science"* will perhaps be surprised by the manner and method employed in the present one. We owe them a few preliminary words of explanation.

The assertions of science and philosophy are in the last resort reducible to verifiable facts or to facts and reasoning that can be tested by anyone; they are subject to rational methods of apprehension or proof. Theology, which is the ordered and considered expression of the Church's doctrine, often relies upon reasoning and may make use of factual data, but the truth of its assertions is ultimately based on other assertions which, for it, replace facts—the assertions of Revelation and Tradition interpreted by the Church's teaching. Theology is a science; it has a subject and a method of its own; it reasons and, when occasion requires, it provides proof; but it starts from a premise which is received from an authority and admitted, as an absolute starting point, only by those who have faith.

Theology, then, differs from rational disciplines by its method; but it also differs from them by its subject or content. Science is concerned with the thing-in-itself, with its internal structure; it seeks an *explanation* for everything that falls within man's experience. Philosophy, in so far as it is a form of wisdom, seeks an explanation of things in general (what knowledge is, what life is, and so forth); but also, and primarily, it is concerned with the *meaning* of things for man. This aspect has been particularly developed in what is called the philosophy of values, where the subject is, not bare facts, but the appraisal of facts. Theology has nothing positive to say on the technical aspects of the race question; except for what the Bible can tell us—and we shall speak of that later—it does not have to teach us what race is, what races there are, or what the present or past relationship between races is or has been—all of which are questions that science tries to answer. But, taking as its basis God's word propounded by the Church, theology can tell us what the meaning of race and racism is for man—man as spoken of in the Revelation, that is to say, man made in the image of God and called to the communion of the Father in Jesus Christ. This is all that the present booklet will attempt to do.

The question is not altogether a simple one. There is racism, and there are the facts of race. Racism, carried to its logical conclusion, is a doctrinal tenet, a theoretical rationalization and so-called justification of racial prejudice; it takes practical shape in certain more or less violent forms of discrimination. But, as the sub-structure for such a doctrine, there are actual racial facts, mingled in a series of very complex historical contexts. Sometimes the degrees and gradations between those facts and minor measures of discrimination are almost imperceptible. Although extreme forms of racism are easy to condemn and indeed stand self-condemned, the right attitude to adopt in the face of this or that racial fact is obviously far less clear. Here we enter the realm of what is often called, at once correctly and misleadingly, "the Church's social doctrine". This has as its sub-structure a series of immutable principles, which reflect the explicit assertions or the necessary implications of the Revelation. But it also includes practical applications whose development is governed by historical, sociological, economic and cultural facts. There is much variation in these practical applications. The sensitivity of mankind varies, and therefore the sensitivity of Christians, who are not outside history, suspended between Heaven and earth, but have to try, within history, to live their faith in the Lord Jesus. It is obvious, for instance, that the manner of feeling and conceiving the freedom of the act of faith, of consent in marriage or of taking religious vows, has varied between the age of St. Benedict, or Charlemagne, or even Louis XIV, and our own day. On the freedom of individual action, on social pressure, we have views which those periods did not share. Canon Law itself forbids, today, procedures which it formerly allowed. From the point of view of principle, the doctrine has not changed, but there have been changes in its practical application; we may even say that it has developed, because certain needs or practices, which were in fact always inherent in the principles of the Gospel, have with time and circumstance emerged and taken concrete shape. Thus does an individual's psychological personality assert itself as the opportunities and demands of life arise.

It is natural, therefore, that our survey should be divided into two parts. First, there is the plane of principle, in which we shall be led to condemn racism absolutely. Second, there is the plane of racial and historical fact, in which connexion we shall see how Christianity has acted and what its attitude in practice is.

THE OPPOSITION OF THE CHURCH TO THE PRINCIPLE OF RACISM

What is racism? It is the dividing and grading of human beings into groups, and then the effecting of discrimination against some of them, on the ground that their human qualities or characteristics are genetically determined. Racism refuses to see man outside a system of classification based on genetic factors (real or supposed). In its view, it is these factors that radically and decisively qualify, unite or separate men.

This standpoint is incompatible with the tenets of the Christian faith as regards (a) the unity and (b) the dignity of human nature, and also with Christian spirituality. Racism is a pseudo-religion; it has disastrous results which attack Christianity at its roots.

CHRISTIAN ASSERTIONS ON THE UNITY OF HUMAN NATURE

Christianity—one might say Judeo-Christianity, for the Revelation is Judeo-Christian—ascribes complete unity to human nature from beginning to end. For God, who is One, is its beginning and its end. When St. Paul speaks of the unity and universality of salvation, he always recalls the unity of God.[1] The logical conclusion of racism is the practical denial of God and of His Kingdom; it would take us, beyond the prophets of Israel and their claim that God is the universal omnipotent Lord, to the ethnic religions, with their several gods each belonging to one place.

The Fathers took the story of the creation, in Genesis, as signifying the unity of all mankind. Ephraem, Ambrose and Theodoret even observe that this is the meaning of the story showing Eve made from Adam, which we should take, not necessarily as a statement about

---

[1] Cf. Acts XVII, 24 et seq.; Eph. IV, 4-6; I Tim. II, 1-5, Rom. III, 29-30 and X, 12.

anatomy, but as a religious statement illustrating and strengthening the affirmation of the unity of creation, the absolute homogeneity of human nature in man and woman and in all their descendants. This was also what God meant when He said "Let us make man in our image". We know that there are three Persons in God, but only one Godhead; three Persons sharing the same Divine nature, the same goodness, the same omnipotence. . . . Thus man is at the same time one and many; many, if individuals are considered; one, if man's nature is considered, that is to say all the innate qualities by virtue of which individuals, one and all, can be called men.

Christianity affirms unity not only at the beginning; it affirms it at the end, as something towards which the world is moving. A Christian philosopher like Vladimir Soloviev expressed this profoundly, in the true thought of the Fathers, when he spoke of "unitotality" as the purpose of God's plan. Man was made one in the beginning but, as it were, in a unity of solitude. God's plan, with Jesus Christ as its decisive instrument, consists in proceeding from this unity of solitude to a unity of plenitude, developing, in their many and varied forms, the almost infinite potentialities inherent in the human being. It is therefore normal and right that humanity should exist and develop in the form of a multiplicity of races, peoples, cultures and creatures of every kind. Christianity's programme itself wishes it so, for it is a programme of catholicity as well as of unity. Yet without in any way subscribing to neo-platonism, but merely to interpret God's plan as the Revelation discloses it to us, we may say that this plan is to proceed from each to each through the many—from the unity of solitude to the unity of plenitude through a wide range of variations. Man was made one in the beginning; but only in the end, when history has been completely unfolded and all peoples and races have become one in Christ, will it be possible truly to say "Man is made". This thought inspired the English poet Tennyson when, following St. Gregory of Nyssa (and, basically, St. Paul himself, with his conceptions of recapitulation, the pleroma, the Body of Christ), he wrote:

14

Man as yet is being made, and ere the crowning Age of
                                                   [ages,
Shall not aeon after aeon pass and touch him into shape?
All about him shadow still, but, while the races flower and
                                                   [fade,
Prophet-eyes may catch a glory slowly gaining on the
                                                   [shade,
Till the peoples all are one, and all their voices blend in
                                                   [choric
Hallelujah to the Maker "It is finish'd. Man is made".

We now see how Christianity can combine the most
radical affirmation of the unity of human nature with
a definite recognition of the fact of the diversity of races
and peoples (a fact presumed to be one of the findings
of science). Better still: Christianity attaches to the
existence of different peoples, and contingently of different races, not merely a human and earthly value, but
a Christian and providentially intended value. Progress
from unity in solitude to unity in plenitude, which is
the trend of human history, requires it. Unfortunately,
human egotism and pride (from which none is free, for
each of us receives at birth a nature inclined to evil)
ceaselessly transform differences into antagonisms, and
diversities into causes of misunderstanding and fratri-
cidal quarrels (see below, à propos of the Tower of
Babel).

CHRISTIAN ASSERTIONS ON THE DIGNITY OF HUMAN NATURE

If man's nature is one, human dignity is likewise the
same in all men. Equality and fraternity are values that
are part of human nature itself. Ancient philosophy indeed, in its stoic form, came near to recognizing them.
But Christianity gave them a basis, a strength, a refine-
ment and a range that they would not otherwise have
had. It not only affirmed but made it apparent that all
men have the same Creator and Father, the same
Redeemer, the same vocation, the same ultimate hope—
and the same home, which is the Church.
   He who, while saying "Our Father", would deny a
Negro or a Jew the status of a brother, even if only by
implication or as a pure matter of practice, would not
be really invoking the Father who is in Heaven, and he

would not be heard. It is because there is but one God, in whose image all have been fashioned, one Father whose children we all likewise are, that all men are brothers, in a way that no created power can destroy. The only means of denying this brotherhood is to set oneself outside the Fatherhood of God. Here again, the logical conclusion of racism is the abandonment of Christianity.

The brotherhood of man remains a brotherhood in sin, in the need of a mediator to make our peace with God our Father, and in the Redemption of the world by Jesus Christ. He died "not for that nation only, but that also he should gather together in one the children of God that were scattered abroad".[1] Affirmations of the universality of the Redemption abound; there is no statement telling us of the Redemption, that does not speak also of its universality. Here again, the one cannot be contested without contesting the other.

Thus in the realm of the immortal soul—the pre-eminent, though not the most tangible realm—men have the same vocation and the same essential history. From the earthly point of view I might of course say (at least up to a point): "What have I in common with the Laplanders or the Fuegians? My history is not theirs, nor is their history mine." It is clearly somewhat ridiculous to give Indo-Chinese children French textbooks where they will read, for instance; "Our ancestors the Gauls". . . . But we can always give them the Bible and make them say, like German children, "Our father Abraham". For, as Pius XI most truly said, "spiritually we are Semites"; Abraham is our father, because he was the first to be "called", and the first believer. We all have a common history which began with Abraham and is centred on Jesus Christ.

During the last few years it has been clearly shown that what unites men most strongly is a common destiny and a common hope. This is doubtless one of the reasons why it is easy to establish contact with travelling companions, whom one has nevertheless only just met and will soon be leaving. The same is true *a fortiori* of war comrades, comrades in escapes from prison camps, political comrades or comrades in social struggle. With

---

[1] John XI, 52.

16

all Christians—nay, with all men throughout the world—
we share the most complete, profound and crucial of all
common destinies, the destiny of the world's salvation,
of its divine trend; the highest, strongest, most stirring
common hope, the hope of the Kingdom of God. Because
it is not apprehended by our senses, we are scarcely
aware of it. Yet it is so.

For this very reason we must be, we are, banded
together—one and the same Church, which is the earthly
Body of Christ. There is no more a Church for each race
or nation than there is a God for each nation or race;
if, in practice, Christianity admits the existence of
national Churches and recognizes different jurisdictions
and rituals in the same city, according to ethnic groups
(for instance, in Alexandria and Jerusalem), it does so
in acknowledgment of the human factor in God's work.
St. Paul was entirely right when he said in the mystic
Body of Christ there was neither Jew nor Greek, neither
bond nor free;[1] he even added "neither male nor female",
and this shows us the exact meaning of his words. Jesus
said that in Heaven "they neither marry nor are given in
marriage".[2] He also said that there would be, among His
followers here below, some preparation and, as it were,
parables of the Kingdom.[3] If the church were entirely
unsullied by human nature, there would be no difference
within it between man and woman, Greek and Jew. But
here below, it cannot completely free itself from man-
made differentiations. Moreover, by speaking Greek in
Greece and Arabic or Coptic in Egypt, the Church affirms
its transcendence above them all. Yet the Church itself
is "neither Latin, Greek, nor Slav".[4] The Church adapts
itself to peoples and races, and this is also a means
whereby it accomplishes its mission of uniting all in
Jesus Christ; only thus can it rightly claim to be the
Catholic Church. But at no moment can this mean that
there would be a Nordic or Slav Church, a Nordic or
Slav truth. In adapting itself to man the Church must
at no moment become the servant of an egotism dictated
by pride and sectarianism, and thus betray the Gospel.
It seems clear, from all the Gospel tells of Jesus, that if

---

[1] Gal. III, 28.
[2] Matthew XXII, 30.
[3] Matthew XIX, 12.
[4] Benedict XV, *Motu proprio Dei Providentis,* 1 May 1917.

He learnt of the existence of Negro churches to which whites were not admitted, it is to such churches that He would go, and that in Pretoria or Cape Town He would travel in compartments reserved for Indians.

We may be confident that the Catholic Church has generally been faithful to the Gospel, for prophets of Nazi racism like Houston Stewart Chamberlain and Alfred Rosenberg have filled their books with accusations that the Church has destroyed every national growth and all original culture. The Church's ideal, they say, is world uniformity on the unitarian basis of a *volklose Weltkirche*. In particular, the Catholic Church has always opposed the Nordic, Germanic genius!

RACISM IS CONTRARY TO CHRISTIAN SPIRITUALITY

The encyclical *Mit brennender Sorge,* of 14 March 1937, accused Nazi racism of seeking a basis and rule of life for man in race alone.[1] Nordic racial theorists have invoked psychological and moral qualities such as courage, honour, initiative and loyalty. It is extremely significant that the racial theorists (Gobineau, Chamberlain, Rosenberg, Darré) have never been able to say what they meant by race without invoking such qualities, or without gratuitously creating a kind of ideal type far removed from empirical findings or historical fact. The same individual was associated first with one racial group and then with another, on the basis of considerations which, so far from being genetic, were entirely ideological; Louis XIV, for instance, was called anti-Teutonic when he expelled the Protestants, but *echter Germane* when he upheld the prerogatives of the Gallican Church. Yet racism is materialist in this, that it turns the higher realities like art, culture, law and even religion into an expression of the surge and call of the "blood", that is, of genetic factors. The phrases are still fresh in our memory: "Art is always the product of a specific race"; "All true culture is the conscious form taken by the growing life force of a race" (Rosenberg). Then come these terrible blasphemies; "For us, right can only be what serves German honour"; "Right is what is ad-

---

[1] Acta, 1937, p. 158, *et seq.*

vantageous to the *Volk*" (both "people" and "race"); "Faith is closely dependent upon race" (W. Hauer, etc.). We remember the practical results of such ideas; the establishment by the Third Reich of a new type of judicial administration, i.e. judgment not according to a definite law but according to an instinctive appreciation of what the good of the people required (Law of 28 June 1935); the attempt to create and define a Nordic religion; and the savage anti-Semitism which led to Auschwitz and all the other such camps—the greatest crime in the whole of human history.

No country which at present permits racial discrimination professes such erroneous principles. The conclusions of this survey will justify certain forms of discrimination, but not on racial grounds. It may be legitimate—although this is very questionable and much open to abuse—to apply different penal systems in the same country to Europeans, amongst whom corporal punishment has long been abolished, and to the natives, with whom it is still a practice. But (a) in no case can the same action be considered right for one group of people when it is regarded, and regarded by all mankind, as criminal for another; (b) discrimination may be acceptable on grounds of a situation deriving from historical fact, but *never* on the ground of purely racial differences. For instance, conditions of residence for gipsies may be subject to fairly severe restrictions *because* gipsies are a special social group with a particular kind of life or behaviour; but these conditions could not be imposed simply *because* gipsies are of a particular physical type and of a different racial origin. The distinction may sometimes be a difficult one to draw, but it is real and very important.

It is a question of the basis on which, in the last resort, all legislation is justified. If the human lawmaker refuses something because of certain behaviour or because it is unfitting—or if, for example, the ecclesiastical authorities refuse communion to a man because he comes incorrectly dressed, or because he belongs to a prohibited sect—he is not denying a right that is outside his competence; but if he refuses something to a man *because* of the colour of his skin, he is usurping the power of the Divine Lawgiver and is arrogating to himself an authority which he does not possess. For we can only have *authority* in a realm which we have *created*; a human

19

agency has it where the social wealth acquired by human industry, whose common exploitation it regulates, is concerned; it does not have it where the inherent rights of man's elemental nature are concerned, since this it has not created. Such rights lie within the competence of the Creator. And that is why the Church is their guardian; that is why, while recognizing the rightful prerogatives of the State such as it knows to be founded on the Will of God, the Church has always declared legally invalid such legislation as infringes the natural right (older and more fundamental than society's rights) of the human being or the family.[1]

As for religion itself, the linking of it with race is an error that Nordic racial theorists have only been able to sustain by building up, quite arbitrarily and in conflict with the most reliable evidence, a myth of "Aryan religion", ostensibly of an inner and mystical nature, in opposition to a phantom "Semitic religion," of a servile nature and dependent on externals. Man is spiritual or atheist, morally good or bad and not because of his blood, but according to his loyalty to a spiritual instinct placed in his nature by God, and according to his personal response to God's voice speaking to him either within, through his conscience, or without, through the preaching of His apostles.

One statement recurs incessantly in Biblical language, in connexion with the Judeo-Christian religion: that religion comes, not from flesh and blood, but from a twofold impulse from God—outside us, when He speaks his Word to us, and within us, when He inclines us towards that Word through the obedience of faith. This religion, the whole of it, begins with the calling, and the faith, of Abraham and his faith, with the demand that he should "Leave his kindred and his father's house".[2] It will be shown later that the Old Testament has remained true to this initial impulse, despite a superficial appearance of attachment to a single race. At all events, nothing is more clearly confirmed in the New Testament. Communion with God, Jesus proclaims, does not depend on birthplace or physical situation—not even on that, unique and blessed among all others, of being a man's

---

[1] Cf. *Mit brennender Sorge*, pp. 159-60.
[2] Genesis XII, 1.

mother[1]—it depends solely on the faith which each man, in his heart, reposes in the Word that is given to him. Thus it is repeatedly declared that neither flesh nor blood makes us friends of God, but inner obedience to His voice.[2] That is why every man and every race can enter, through Christ, into the communion of God, which is the Holy Church. And indeed the Church does, even visibly, contain in its bosom (which is Abraham's bosom) men of every race; the vision of the Apocalypse,[3] which vindicates the prophecies of the Old Testament, is a vision that may already gladden our earthly eyes.

RACISM IS A PSEUDO-RELIGION

Pope Pius XI proclaimed, in eloquent and truly prophetic words, that by transposing the great premises of Christianity into terms of race, racism was profoundly perverting them and becoming itself a pseudo-religion; this applied alike to the concepts of Revelation, faith, immortality, original sin, Redemption and the Cross, humility, and grace.[4] If there is in Christianity the idea of a mystery of blood, of a community of blood, it is that, not of a race opposed to other races, but of the unity of all men in the heritage of sin, derived from our first father, and in a heritage of Redemption purchased by the blood of Christ.[5] Whenever it is said that a given race—or class—is absolutely sacred, it becomes endowed with the attributes of the Church or the Mystical Body of Jesus Christ. This can easily be seen from a perusal of racist writings or certain writings on class, which proclaim that a man is just and innocent, that he is saved and wins true freedom, that he is the heir of the supreme good and enters into a sort of Communion of Saints if he belongs to a given race or class. But this always excludes others, against whom it is proper and indeed commendable to make war, in which any methods may be employed.

---

[1] Cf. Luke XI, 27-28; Matthew XII, 46-50.
[2] Cf. John I, 13; Matthew XVI, 17; I Corinthians XV, 50; Gal. I, 16; Eph. VI, 12.
[3] Revelation VII, 9.
[4] *Mit brennender Sorge*, pp. 156-58.
[5] Cf. speech by Cardinal van Roey, Archbishop of Malines, 1938.

21

The true Church, the true Mystical Body, are open to all men; the battle they wage is the battle of the Spirit and their only weapons are the weapons of light; their law is that of the universal merciful love proceeding from the heart of God.

RACISM HAS DISASTROUS CONSEQUENCES FOR CHRISTIANITY

Any form of racism—not only absolute, systematized racism, but also pragmatic and comparatively moderate racism—has disastrous consequences running counter both to the spirit and to the letter of Christianity.

Racism and Eugenics

The Catholic Church does not condemn eugenics whole-sale, but it has taken a firm and uncompromising stand against all forms of eugenics which do not respect the absolute value of human life and which treat man, in practice, simply as an animal species, a subject for zootechny. It is not entirely honest nor truly intelligent to deal with the Church's action and prohibitions in this field without reference to the general principles which guide them. Yet this is precisely what such writers as Paul Blanshard do. The Church has no idea of prohibiting all eugenic practices or research. It has its own point of view, governed by its unshakable refusal to treat human affairs as pertaining purely to the physical world or to consider them apart from the special quality, vocation and spiritual resources of man. The Church preaches man's responsibility for his actions, the dignity of sexual matters and procreation, and the pre-eminence of the supernatural virtues. It holds that, even on the animal side of his nature, man is not an animal; his senses, which pertain to his animal nature, are yet not the senses of an animal but of man, being subordinate to human and spiritual ends. This is overlooked not only by racist doctrine but also by that unconsciously materialistic attitude towards eugenics that racial feeling inspires—especially in those sections of a society which feel themselves to be threatened because they lack vitality and moral health.

The attitude of the Catholic Church towards the

question of sterilization has gradually developed with the passage of time. This is probably one of the matters which might illustrate the idea, put forward by such jurists as G. Renard, of "natural law with a developing content". We said above that the "social doctrine of the Church" is itself of this type and develops gradually, through the reactions of Christian feeling, holding fast to abiding principles, to the facts of history in given conditions. The Church's present attitude on this point, as sanctioned by the ordinary Magisterium,[1] may be summarized as follows:

1. No individual has the right to have himself rendered sterile except to save his life—not, for instance, to be able to indulge in carnal pleasure without undertaking the responsibilities of procreation. Any system of law which legalized sterilization, subject only to the consent of the person concerned, would thus fail to satisfy the Church's requirements, based on its interpretation of those of natural law.

2. An individual has the right voluntarily to renounce the *exercise* of his power of procreation. Such renunciation may indeed be a moral duty (vow of celibacy or virginity; obligation of limiting the number of births; responsibility for not perpetuating a tainted strain).

3. Society (the State) has at times assumed the right to sentence those guilty of certain very serious crimes to suffer mutilation in this way as a punishment or possibly as a precaution against a repetition of the crime. The encyclical *Casti connubii* gives no ruling on this point. The progress of moral thought, however, seems to be excluding this practice from the laws of civilized countries. Some Catholic writers (such as Father Agapito Marin de Sobradillo) consider that the State might forbid certain individuals

---

[1] Main references: The encyclical *Casti connubii* of 31 December 1930 (*Acta Apostolicæ Sedis*, 1930, pp. 562 *et seq.*) and Decree of the Holy Office, dated 21 March 1931 (*Acta Apostolicæ Sedis*, 1931, pp. 118-19); the reactions of German and Italian Catholics (cf. *Documentation catholique*, Paris, Vol. 30, 1933, col. 683-99, 817-28, and Vol. 31, 1934, col. 430-31); Decree of the Holy Office, prohibiting "direct" sterilization, i.e. sterilization desired for its own sake and not, for instance, as a means of saving life, 24 February 1940 (*Acta Apostolicæ Sedis*, 32, 1940, p. 73); Decree of the Holy Office, dated 2 December 1940, condemning eugenic murder (*Acta Apostolicæ Sedis*, 32, 1940, p. 553).

the right to marry and have children, when necessary in the interests of the common weal. Others are absolutely against any such idea.[1]

4. The State is not entitled to deprive an individual of his procreative power simply for material (eugenic) purposes. But it is entitled to isolate individuals who are sick and whose progeny would inevitably be seriously tainted.

5. True eugenics is a matter involving the solution of the social problem (slums, drunkenness, prostitution, pauperism), the general respect of ethics, training in the sense of responsibility and the spirit of providence, constructive health legislation (especially for the benefit of children born of handicapped parents but who are not necessarily handicapped themselves) and the spread of the practice of sports. The Catholic attitude must be considered as a whole. It does not pronounce certain prohibitions without suggesting constructive means of promoting a healthy life. If God's law were observed, the aims of eugenics would very largely be achieved.

The Destruction of Brotherly Love

Any form of racism, even in modified guise, attacks the very heart of Christianity, which is love. It attacks the very concept of our "neighbour"—the name used to designate other people in Christian parlance, which is that of charity or love.

We all know the Bible story of the lawyer who, having truly set forth the law of love, but wishing to justify himself, asked Jesus "And who is my neighbour?" Jesus answered: "A certain man went down from Jerusalem to Jericho and fell among thieves, who left him half dead. A certain priest chanced to come that way and passed by on the other side; likewise also a Levite. But a certain Samaritan, coming where he was, went to him and took care of him. Which now of these three," asked Jesus, "thinkest thou, was neighbour unto him that fell among thieves?" The lawyer replied: "He that showed mercy on him. . . ."[2] There is a very profound meaning

---

[1] *Osservatore Roma,* 13 August 1933.
[2] Luke X, 25-37.

in this parable. It is obvious that Jesus does not mean that we must love our neighbour, in the sense of those who show us kindness. He expressly describes such an attitude as typical of the publicans rather than of the disciples, whom He exhorts to imitate their Father which is in Heaven, who "maketh His sun to rise on the evil and on the good".[1] Jesus undoubtedly wished to teach, first of all, that our neighbour is he whom God sets in our way, not the friend of our own choice but the stranger we chance across, the man we run into without being able to avoid him, whom God gives us to love. Moreover, Jesus shows the lawyer, by His parable, that his neighbour is not the priest or the Levite, not a man of his own group, his own class, his own world, not a man of his race, but a Samaritan, a man of mixed blood, belonging to a despised people with whom the Jews had no dealings.[2] In point of fact, our neighbour is not he who is bound to us by blood, by affinity or by membership of the same group, but he who is brought near to us by a generous and all-merciful love. That is why Christians speak of other people as their "neighbours".

Race prejudice, however, and still more racism as a theory, implies not love but contempt and distrust of *others*, of people not of the group. People working in the colonies have been unfavourably criticized for their lack of appreciation of "the other man's point of view.[3] The race theorist carries this "colonial" mentality to the extreme and into every sphere. And as there is no more unthinking passion than a group prejudice against another group, and as nothing is easier than to associate contempt or prejudice with some physical detail or feature of the outward behaviour of others, the racist becomes the slave of a psychological complex which undermines the very foundations of love in him. St. John, the apostle of love, tells us: "Whosoever hateth his brother is a murderer."[4] That is very true. It is impossible to hate a man, or simply to despise him, without, sooner or later, finding in our inmost heart some such thought as "People like that ought not to be alive!"

---

[1] Matthew V, 43-48.
[2] Cf. John IV, 9.
[3] O. Mannoni, *Psychologie de la Colonisation*, Paris, Éditions du Seuil, 1950.
Cf. John III, 15.

And Dostoievsky, with his genius, has shown us in the character of Smerdiakov in *The Brothers Karamazov* that such a thought is at the origin of murder.

Anti-Semitism

Race prejudice and, especially, systematized racism almost always leads to anti-Semitism. This is the second way in which it strikes at the heart of Christianity.

Here again, events have made the Church and many Christians, including the present writer, see more clearly, and with greater depth and purity the real significance and implication of their doctrinal principles. N. Berdiaeff remarked very truly in 1938 that "the forms of persecution to which the Jews are at present being subjected lead, from the Christian point of view, to the final condemnation of anti-Semitism. This is to be regarded as a good consequence of Nazi racism" The immeasurable sufferings of Israel seem to have been, as it were, the mysterious condition for a better understanding of Israel's place in God's scheme and for an illuminating and profoundly fruitful rediscovery of what the Old Testament means to Christianity itself. The ancient Church in its early days already realized clearly that, as it was the "new Israel" "accomplishing" the old, it could deny nothing of that old Israel. This fact is all the more remarkable because, at that time, the Christian Church was gaining strength in opposition to the Synagogue and was engaged in controversy with the Jews. When Marcion, however, attempted to rid the New Testament of all things pertaining to the Old, the Church cast him out, thus affirming its deep awareness of the impossibility of being the Church of Christ except as the heir of Israel. That is also the reason why the efforts of Nordic racism to contrast an inward and mystical "Aryan" religion with a "Semitic" religion of a God in the guise of creator and ruler were bound to appear to the Church simply as absurd lucubrations.

For a Christian, to defend anti-Semitism is to deny in practice that Israel cannot be a people like others but is always the object of divine election—the agonizing contradiction of being still God's Israel and, at the same time, no longer the "true Israel". Here we are no longer concerned simply with that destruction of love of which we have already spoken, but with something peculiar to Israel, which also lies at the very heart of Chistianity. We shall see, in the second part of this study, what are the practical sociological and political problems that the nations—Christian and otherwise—are faced with as a consequence of the survival of Jewish communities in their midst. They are real problems, although often exaggerated and sophisticated by a regrettable lack of calm and indeed of impartiality. The mistake is to see nothing but those problems, to regard the Hebrew community only as *Jews*, not as *Israel* (to use a distinction in terms which we find in the Bible itself).[1] Such an attitude leads to two very serious errors; the first lies in failing to recognize the spiritual problem, in losing sight and consciousness of it beneath the human, sociological or political problem; the second lies in treating the human problem itself in purely physical terms, that is, in non-human and *a fortiori* in non-Christian terms. "The existence of the Jews in a country may give rise to a problem or problems. However that may be, no Christian is entitled to approach those problems with an anti-Semitic outlook."[2]

If the mystery of Israel were reduced to the sociological or political problem of the Jews (a problem which, itself, is incorrectly stated), Christians would run the risk of reducing Catholicism to a sociological phenomenon, a social religion. This danger is clearly apparent in such writers as Charles Maurras. As the "Jewish danger" has been removed by purely political measures, Christianity itself has lost its "virulence". For the prophetic energy which flows through the Church has its source in the people who looked for the fulfilment of God's promise, in the people distinguished by Messianism and eschatology, in the people "who brought into man's consciousness the very category of the historical"

---

[1] *Hebrew* is a purely ethnological term (meaning "passer-over" or "immigrant"). *Jew*, derived from "Judaean, Judah", designates tne people as a purely earthly and human group; the word is used in the Scriptures and in secular writings when the Jews are referred to as a political entity, or as traders, etc.; in St. John's Gospel, the "Jew" is the man who has rejected Jesus. *Israelite* designates the Jewish people from the religious standpoint, the people of the Revelation and of the Covenant (cf. von Rod and Gutbrod, "Israël" in Kittel's *Woerterbuch*, Vol. III, especially p. 357 *et seq.* and p. 378 *et seq.*).
[2] Y. de Montcheuil, December 1940, in *L'Eglise et le Monde Actuel*, p. 106.

(N. Berdiaeff). It is of course regrettable, in some respects, that Israel, by failing to fulfil its election in Christ, secularized as it were its peculiar vocation of supplying the prophetic leaven to the lump. It is for that reason that Karl Marx, despite his bitter criticism of money-making Jewry, is so essentially a Jew; it is for that reason that there is so often a disturbing revolutionary element in what the Jews do. Nevertheless, their peculiar vocation is to be called *for* the nations, *pars pro toto*, "a minority in the service of a majority" (J. Weill). They can be understood, even from the standpoint of human history, only if we view them in this light.

Even more clearly, therefore, we cannot hope to reach and preserve the very heart of Christianity unless we respect what it has inherited from its Jewish forerunners, and hence, unless we treat the remnants of unbelieving Israel which are to be found among all the other peoples as the fragments of a Chosen Vessel whereby the highest gifts of God have come to us.

IS THE BIBLE RACIST?

But were not the Jews themselves the first exponents of racial doctrine? Do not we read in the Bible of one blessing, reserved to them, and of curses directed against other races as such? We must therefore reconsider the racial pronouncements of the Scriptures and the element of racism in the phenomenon of Israel as a "chosen people".

One point is clear at the outset: the election was certainly that of a people, but neither in the content nor in the significance of God's choice was there any element of racism. It is noteworthy that the religion of Israel differs profoundly from that of other peoples of the same racial community, which makes the Nazi proposition of a close link and an exact correspondence between race and religion pure invention. Israel was chosen *as a people* because God's purpose is to unite all men in a single spiritual people, the Church, to save them and lead them to communion with Him, not in isolation but as a community. Israel was thus chosen for and on behalf of all, *pars pro toto*. If the choice fell, in the first place, upon *one* people alone, it was because it is apparently God's pleasure to give first to one or to a few what He intends for all, so that men's efforts and advances throughout history may become a part of His scheme of universal mercy. It was also in order to shelter the newly planted seed of true religion and to protect the young plant before it was exposed to all the winds of the world's civilization.

That there was no racist significance in God's choice—that the Bible, when it talks of a "chosen people", has no thought of a superior race or a *Herrenvolk*—is clearly and explicitly stated. We are told, in fact, that Israel was chosen not because of any superior qualities—how much the Greeks excelled the Jews in that respect!—but precisely because they had no such qualities.[1] This significance of Divine election is brought out in all the books of the Bible by the fact that God constantly reverses relative positions, choosing the younger in place of the elder—as in the stories of Cain and Abel, Jacob and Esau, Ephraim and Manasseh, and David—or taking barren women for the mothers of the chief of the elect among His people—as Sarah, Rebecca, Samson's mother, Hannah the mother of Samuel, Elizabeth the mother of John the Baptist. Thus the "chosen people" does not mean a privileged, exceptionally gifted race; there is no idea of racism in the choice of God's people.

Nor is there any idea of racism in the content of the election. Throughout, from the very beginning, Israel is chosen for all mankind, to be the medium of a Revelation designed for all. The idea of God which emerges from the Bible differs profoundly from that found among all the other peoples surrounding the Israel of those times, in that Yahweh is not the god of a particular people, associated, like the particular gods, with a given group of men. He is the Creator of all things; there are no other gods beside Him. That, too, is why He is not bound to a particular place, such as a mountain, a spring, or a sanctuary. This point is very clearly brought out by Stephen, in his speech before the Sanhedrin, and by Paul, in his speech before the Areopagus.[2] This gives us a clearer understanding of the meaning of the two passages in which the Bible speaks of the division of

---

[1] See Deut. VII, 7; cf. X, 14-15; Ezek. XVI, 3-15; I Cor. I, 27.
[2] Acts VII and XVII, 22 *et seq.*

29

the races, i.e. the generations of Noah, leading on to the story of the Tower of Babel.[1] The author of a recent study on the story of the Creation, M. W. Zimmerli[2] notes that the two stories are complementary. The story which explains the diversity of the peoples descended from Noah shows us the happy, positive aspect of that diversity. Happy is the man who has many descendants. There is *nothing* in the Bible reflecting on the Negroes as the "accursed sons of Ham"; the theocratic writers who, like Joseph de Maistre, claimed to know, from the Bible, what was God's opinion of the history of their times, and above all those who, like some British and American writers of the eighteenth and nineteenth centuries, used the Bible to justify the slave-trade, were guilty of a complete misinterpretation and read into Holy Writ something which was never there at all. There is in the Scriptures no curse pronounced against any race, as such.

From the standpoint of biblical Revelation, it is natural for mankind to be one or, at all events, to live together in peace and harmony. If diversity among men leads to conflict and impossibility of agreement, it is something unnatural for which an explanation must be found. The Bible explains it by the etiological account of the Tower of Babel, which shows the harmful aspect of the diversity —in itself neither good nor bad but, on the whole, fortunate in its effects—between races, peoples and languages. From the story itself, the racial, political and linguistic unity of mankind is not, in itself, reprehensible. God opposes that unity only when it inspires the presumptuous ambition of eluding His sovereignty. E. König, who has brought this out clearly,[3] also notes[4] that no other ancient literature lays so much stress as the Bible upon the unity of mankind. He shows[5] that, from the creation of Adam onwards, the Bible contemplates a plan on the part of God, and a history of salvation, for the whole of humanity. Even after the fall, God refrains from destroying man; He has given him pledges of His

---

[1] Gen. X, 1; XI, 9.
[2] *1 Mose 1-11, Die Urgeschichte*, Zürich, 1943; more particularly, Vol. II, pp. 170-235.
[3] *Theologie des Alten Testaments*, § 13, Stuttgart, 1922, pp. 53-54.
[4] *Ibid.*, p. 51.
[5] *Ibid.* and § 77, pp. 259-69.

love, certain means of knowing Him; He has, as it were, entered into a compact with mankind to show man mercy and endow him with the gifts of nature. Even when the pride of men has drawn upon them the curse of Babel, God, though transferring His plan of grace to one family and one people, by the election of Abraham, does not fail to announce explicitly, from the beginning, the universalist purpose of what He is doing: "In thee shall all families of the earth be blessed."

This universalist design is never entirely lacking in the history of Israel. Before the Gentiles entered the Church and the confusion of Babel was made good by the miracle of Pentecost, there was a sort of anticipation and pledge of universal salvation, an assimilation to God's people of individuals of different ethnic stocks— Rahab, the harlot of Jericho; Abimelech, the son of Gideon and a Canaanitish woman; Ruth the Moabitess, who was one of the ancestors of Jesus; and the great anonymous multitude of those who were admitted to the religious communion of Israel as proselytes (a word which, it may be said in passing, is peculiar to biblical language—a fact not without significance).[1] It is impossible, in this context, to omit mention of the splendid expressions of the universalist outlook which are to be found, in numbers, in the Psalms and the Prophets from the time of the Exile onwards. We cannot quote them here, but they should be re-read in Isaiah XI, 9; XIV, 1-2; XIX, 19-25; XLIX, 18-23; LII, 10 et seq.; LVI, 1-8; LXVI, 18-21; Ps. 2, 7-8; 22, 27-28; 65, 1-2; 67, 1-2; 72, 8-11; 86, 8-10; 96, 5, 7, 10; 98, 6-7; Zech. II, 11-13; VIII, 20-23; XIV, 20-21; Joel III, 1-2; Malachi, I, 11; etc. So far as the Bible is concerned, all the peoples are at fault, but they are all covered by God's forgiveness and they shall all come to Him.

However, there are also in the Scriptures commandments to destroy members of other races, or indeed to destroy those races in general. In the thousand years that elapsed between the command to destroy the Midianites, the Canaanites, etc. of which we read in the Book of Numbers, Deuteronomy or Joshua, and the somewhat similar measures taken by Ezra after the Exile, much blood was shed. But it is clear, and indeed stated

---

[1] See Exodus XII, 48-49.

explicitly in the Bible, that strange peoples and strange wives were never condemned to destruction as a result of race discrimination as such, but were so condemned because of the danger or the actual commission of idolatry.[1] Nor was it racial prejudice, as such, which inspired so many of the measures for the protection of the line of the Patriarchs, and later of that of Judah, but rather the desire to remain pure for the carrying out of God's purpose, which was, from Abraham to Mary, through Judah and David, to fulfil the messianic promises.

There could thus be no greater error than to interpret the Old Testament in terms of race and, more especially, of racism. Even after the rise of Christianity, Judaism, scattered but still indivisible, never gave a racist interpretation of its position. There may have been a spontaneous tendency in that direction among the people, and that tendency may have been strengthened to the extent that the Jews themselves secularized the idea of their people and, to use the terms we explained above, became "Jews" rather than "Israelites". In some parts of the Talmud itself, universalism is, here and there, practically abandoned and God's choice is regarded as the choise of Israel for its own sake rather than for all mankind. That is not enough to constitute racism. On the other hand, no one was ever definitively excluded from the community of Israel on the ground that he was not descended, after the flesh, from Abraham. Not only individuals of Aryan stock but entire ethnic groups have been received into that community (e.g. the Chazars from south of the Volga, from the ninth to the eleventh centuries, when they were destroyed; or the Judaized Berbers of North Africa). It often happens, however, that when a given group is treated on a race basis the group itself grows racially conscious, and reacts accordingly; examples of this are to be found among the Negroes in more than one part of Africa. The Jews probably followed a similar line of development here and there. If this is true, they would not, at all events, have been the first exponents of a racist doctrine.

---

[1] Cf. Numbers XXV, 5; Deut. IX, 4; Ezra IX, 1 *et seq.*

THE PRACTICAL POLICY OF THE CHURCH WITH REGARD TO THE FACTS OF RACE

THE RACIAL POINT OF VIEW IS FOREIGN TO THE CATHOLIC TRADITION

The very principles of Christianity were, from the outset, a denial of race prejudice. Moreover, Christianity came into being and first spread in the Graeco-Roman world and within the Roman Empire, which included a variety of races and, as the modern Nordic race theorists have said time and again, professed no race doctrine. The Empire of Augustus, the *Pax Romana*, the *Orbis Romanus* were all fundamentally aracial. The Stoic philosophy, in which the Latins found an ideal which made a natural appeal to them, proclaimed the unity of mankind and the principles of equality and brotherhood among men. The Church thus remained untouched by race prejudice. The Fathers of the Church loved to emphasize this miracle of Christian unity, which embraced so many different men and peoples. "He who is in Rome knows that the Indians are very members of the same body. What society can be compared with this? And all have one Head, which is Christ. . . ."[1]

When, through the conversion of monarchs and their peoples, Christianity developed into a political and legal "Christian Republic" as well as a spiritual Church, when the spiritual authority acquired the means of influencing society, the opposition of Christians towards other groups —heretics or infidels—often resulted in conflict, and sometimes in oppression. Examples which come to mind are the violence to which the Jews were sometimes subjected, the wars against the Moors, the Crusades against Islam, the wars of the Teutonic Knights against the Balts and the Slavs, and the struggle against the Turks. It is a very striking fact, however, that no race sentiment entered into any of these struggles. The sense of division

---

[1] St. John Chrysostom, St. Augustine, etc.

was felt not on that plane, but on the spiritual plane of faith, the conflict being between true belief and false beliefs.[1] The Moors were thought of not as "Arabs" but as "infidels". It is well to note, in this connexion, that the famous expression *perfidia judaïca* probably had not the moral connotation suggested by a misleading transcription of the phrase into modern languages, but was used in the theological and canonical sense, close to the etymological meaning, of unbelief or refusal to believe.[2]

This is not the place to give even a very brief historical sketch of Christian anti-Semitism; it is enough to note that, where it has been found, the underlying reason for it has sometimes been economic or psychological, though more often religious, rather than any considerations of racism.

Within Christendom, there was no racial feeling in the form of chauvinistic nationalism. Nowadays we can more easily recognize the signs of national feeling which made themselves apparent in Europe from Carolingian times onwards, but at the same time we cannot but be impressed by the universality of a Church and a culture through whose influence the University of Paris was able, in the thirteenth century, to boast the Englishman Alexander of Hales, the German Albertus Magnus, and the Italians Thomas Aquinas and Bonaventura; through whose influence also "in the twelfth century, the See of Canterbury was occupied by an Italian, St. Anselm; that of Lincoln by a Savoyard, St. Hugh; that of Chartres by an Englishman, John of Salisbury. . . ."[3]

The results of this universalism, incidentally, were not always entirely good. Roman universality sometimes involved too much uniformity, too much submission, too much neglect of proper national particularities. Several schisms were encouraged by national, sometimes almost racial sentiment, which was too often overlooked; examples are the African schisms of the fourth century

---

[1] Cf. R. F. Benedict, *Race and Racism,* London, The Labour Book Service, 1943, p. 107.

[2] On this question, we may refer not only to scientific studies (E. Peterson, "Perfidia judaica", in *Ephemerides Liturgicæ,* 1936, pp. 296-311; J.-M. Oesterreicher, "Pro perfidis Judaeis", in *Theological Studies,* March 1947, pp. 80 *et seq.*) but also to an official statement of the Congregation of Rites, which authorizes the translations "unbelief, refusal to believe" (*Acta Apostolicæ Sedis,* 1948, p. 342).

[3] Mgr. Feltin, pastoral letter, 1952.

(Donatists and Circumcellions); later on, Czech national sentiment was to find expression in the movement of the Bohemian Brethren, the claims of the Utraquists (demanding the cup in the Eucharist), and the work of John Hus; in the same way, Luther's reforming movement has the background of German national sentiment in revolt against the exactions of Rome and the contemptuous dominion of the Italians. All this shows that the Church, while affirming and achieving a higher unity, has to take into account the facts of nationhood and, if need be, of race. Truth lies in the harmonizing of the principle of universality with the facts of national life.[1] It is possible that, if a Berber Church had developed in North Africa, Islam would have encountered greater resistance.

The few writers who have traced the history of racist ideas are unanimous in telling us that "racial prejudice came into being in the sixteenth century, during the colonial period . . . and even then the phenomenon was not of sudden appearance. It is to be noted that, in the eyes of sixteenth-century men, the spread of Christianity or, in other words, of the dominant form of civilization, ruled out any racial discrimination".[2] "European expansion overseas set the stage for racist dogmas and gave violent early expression to racial antipathies without propounding racism as a philosophy".[3] There seems to be no doubt that racial prejudice is linked, in origin and development, with colonial imperialism. We find eloquent testimony in support of this fact in the development of feeling towards coloured people, and particularly towards Negroes, in England. In the eighteenth century, Negroes were living in England as servants, under a paternalistic system, without arousing any repulsion. It was in the nineteenth century and the twentieth, with the growth of imperialist pride and the development of colonialism, that a feeling of contempt for the Negro grew up in England.[4]

The prejudice typical of colonialism developed in a

---

[1] Cf. Fr. Dvornik, *National Churches and the Church Universal,* Westminster, 1944.
[2] Ch.-A. Julien, "Le Racisme et l'Union Française", in *Mondes d'Orient,* Nos. 9, 10 and 11.
[3] R. F. Benedict, *op. cit.,* p. 111.
[4] Cf. K. L. Little, *Negroes in Britain. A Study of Racial Relations in English Society,* London, Kegan Paul, 1948.

particularly virulent form among certain Spaniards after the discovery and conquest of America. Solorzano informs us, in his *De Indiarum jure*, that many of them denied that the Indians were men although they appeared to be so, on the ground that they had no intelligence. Pietro d'Anghiera, Francisco Lopez de Gomara, Pedro de Cieza de Leon, Girolamo Benzoni (a Milanese), Antonio de Herrera, Simon Maiolus, and Father Gregorio Garcia —in spite of the fact that the latter was a colleague of that admirable man, Las Casas—reiterated throughout the sixteenth century a slogan which enabled them to keep the Indians in *encomienda,* or, in other words, in a state very little removed from that of slavery. It was at this stage that Pope Paul III, informed of the situation by the Dominican, Julio Garcez, Bishop of Tlaxcala, published a series of Bulls, in May and June 1537, which are probably the first pronouncements of the Roman Magisterium on race questions:

"It has come to our mind that our dear son in Christ, Charles, Emperor of the Romans and King of Castille and Leon, published an edict against those who, inflamed by greed, were showing inhumanity towards humankind, which same edict forbade his subjects to reduce the Indians of the West and the South to slavery or to deprive them of their goods. Considering that the Indians themselves, though still not received into the bosom of the Church, are not, and must not be, deprived of their freedom or their possessions, since they are men, and therefore capable of faith and of salvation, and must not be reduced to slavery but, by preaching and example, exhorted to life . . . (there follows an excommunication, reserved to the Holy See, against any who reduce the Indians to slavery or deprive them of their goods).[1]

"The enemy of the human race has suggested to some of his followers the idea of spreading through the world the opinion that the inhabitants of the West Indies and the southern continents, of whose existence we have but recently learnt, should be treated like animals that have not reason, and be employed solely for our profit and our service, on the pretext that they have no part in the Catholic faith and are incapable of adopting it.

---

[1] Bull or Brief *Pastorale officium,* addressed to Cardinal Juan de Tavera, Archbishop of Toledo, on 29 May 1538.

"We, the unworthy Vicar of Our Lord, have to do all that lies within Our power to preserve the flock committed to Our care, and to bring into safety the lost sheep. We regard the Indians as true men, being not only capable of adopting the Christian faith but desirous of doing so.

"Therefore, in the desire of remedying the ill which has been caused, We decide and declare by this Our letter (whose translation shall be authenticated with his seal by every priest) that the aforesaid Indians, and all other peoples which may, in future, become known to Christendom, shall not be deprived of their freedom and their goods—notwithstanding contrary assertions—even if they be not Christians; but that, on the contrary, they shall be left in the enjoyment of their freedom and their property.

"The Indians and other peoples which may yet be discovered in the future shall be converted only by the Word of God and by the example of a good and holy life."[1]

The following year, in his homilies on temperance, and again in 1539 in his *De Indis*,[2] the Dominican, Francisco de Vittoria, established that, as the Indians were men, the same natural law applied to them as applied in Spain. In a world whose horizons had suddenly expanded, and faced with the new factor introduced by the coexistence of Europeans and coloured peoples—faced too, with the first pretensions of a crude and violent colonialism—the Church's position was clearly stated: the Indians, and the black- or yellow-skinned peoples, are men *like the Europeans*. Neither natural law, nor faith, nor salvation recognizes the racial barrier.

The very concept of *race*, incidentally, was at that time far more implicit than explicit. In seventeenth century French, the word was used only in the sense of *lineage*, the family considered as a continuing line of individuals (see Littré). It was not until after the missionary and mercantile age of the great discoveries—when study began on ethnology and comparative religion and, later, on zoology, during the eighteenth century—that the word

---

[1] The Bull *Sublimis Deus*, of 2 June 1537 (some give the date as 9 June). Another Bull, *Veritas Ipsa*, of the same date, addressed to the Discalced Friars, set forth the same ideas.

[2] Getino, Madrid, 1934.

"race" itself was used in reference to peoples. The idea of race had scarcely been introduced into the natural sciences when the philosophers laid hold on it; and later the politicians, after the Romantic age, took it up for their own purposes. Voltaire made use of it to refute Rousseau's idea of the natural unity and original equality of men. Kant was probably the first to give an exact definition of race, as a concept henceforth to be counted among the acquisitions of human thought.[1]

THE CHURCH AND PRESENT-DAY RACISM

Ideas on the subject having thus arrived at some degree of maturity, three major groups of facts distinctive of the nineteenth century brought up the race question in a new and sometimes very acute form, calling for a practical stand by Christian thought. These were: the development of the missionary movement; the colonial conquests which necessarily led to the need for Europeans and natives to live side by side, followed by the anti-slavery movement and all its consequences; and Romantism, followed by the growth of the myth of a particularly attractive and gifted Nordic race, which was later taken up, on a pseudo-scientific basis, by the prophets of Aryan supremacy. Thus we shall see the Church brought face to face, in practice, with (a) the problems arising out of the missionary movement; (b) the questions to which the need for white and coloured people to live side by side has given rise, especially in South Africa and in the United States of America; (c) Nazi racial doctrines and modern anti-Semitism.

The Church and the Races from the Standpoint of the Church's Missionary Work

Missionary work can mean only the introduction of converts into the Apostolic Church, and the establishment of the Church of the Apostles in places and among peoples where it has not previously been known, by

---

[1] *Bestimmung des Begriffs einer Menschenrasse,* 1785, *Werke,* Vol. IV p. 225.

rendering present and active the three great elements which form the structure of the Church; the faith, the sacraments of faith, and the powers of the ministry (priesthood, episcopacy). Both in distant missions and in countries which have long been converted to Christianity, however, the Church necessarily carries out the secondary mission of spreading Christian civilization. Facts throughout history show clearly that the Church has never, in the slightest degree, subscribed to the racist tenet that to pursue such an endeavour is sheer folly, since the pagan peoples are doomed by race to be inferior.[1] Wherever the Church has carried the Gospel, it has also carried—in preparation, as a concomitant, or as a natural outcome—education, care for the sick or undernourished body, a higher status for women, a healthier family existence, consideration for children and for human life, work and respect for work, rules of justice, rules to govern peaceful relations, and so forth.

In short, the first characteristics of Catholic missionary work are the practical demonstration of unity and an enormous enrichment of the recipient peoples. The Church is one, the Church *has much to give*.

But there are other characteristics on the other side of the picture: diversity and the enrichment of the Church. The Church *has much received* from missions; it draws its strength not only from a heavenly source, the Christ, the Second Adam, full of grace and truth, but also from an earthly source, mankind, which is but the substance—multiplied and distributed throughout all peoples, all civilizations, all languages and all the experience of history—of the First Adam, which is to be "resumed" in the Second. The proper place for a justification of the part which the diversity of peoples, and possibly of races, may play in the Church is a theology of catholicity (as we have explained elsewhere[2]). We have already touched on this point above.

Obviously, what we are really concerned with here is the people, i.e. a phenomenon belonging to the world of history and culture—not, in the strict sense, to that of biology. Racist writers constantly fall into the fallacy of passing from one order to another and of attributing to

---

[1] Hitler, *Mein Kampf*, p. 446.
[2] *Chrétiens désunis*, Paris, 1937, Chapter 3.

a more or less mythical entity, which they call race, a variety of features which are really due to historical or local conditions or result from cultural or historical factors. The idea of "race" is not a concept stemming from the Catholic tradition, and has no place in theology, missiology, pastoral theology or canon law. All that the Church can do in this field is to take note, where appropriate, of the conclusions of science. After all, since all spiritual souls are equal, but one individual nevertheless differs from another in intelligence and character by reason of a different balance or a different degree of perfection in his bodily powers, and since those bodily aptitudes are in part inherited and genetically determined, why should not a group of men derived from a common stock at a more or less distant date display a special type of temperament, conditioned by heredity and therefore racial in nature? There is nothing inherently impossible in this; the difficulty is that intermarriage has taken place almost everywhere on so large a scale that the reality of race is extremely problematical. There is no doubt that what we should speak of is not "races" but "peoples".

The demands facing "missiology" (which is itself merely a branch of ecclesiology) as a result of the diversity of peoples and civilizations have generally been dealt with under the heading of "adaptation". A bibliography of the literature on this question would, in itself, fill a booklet such as this. The idea of adaptation, however, does not go far enough. It implies a somewhat paternalistic condescension which, though praiseworthy enough within its proper limits, cannot embody the full ideal of catholicity. On the other hand, people have come much closer to that ideal when they have talked of the native Church, native clergy, native art or even native theology. The problem is not simply to give the countries to which the Gospel is taken a clergy properly "adapted" to their task, familiar with the local language and customs, the forms of art which will make an appeal, and a good translation of the catechism (an enormous problem in itself!); it is also to inspire and strengthen the vocation in the peoples of India, China and the Cameroons, and likewise an art, a system of thought, an embodiment in culture of apostolic Catholicism, which shall be truly Indian, Chinese or Cameroon, just as our own traditions are French—or English, Slav or Spanish.

The main efforts have been devoted to the key problem—that of the native clergy. From the very beginning of missionary work in distant fields, the Popes urged the need for a native clergy and native bishops[1] as did the Congregation *De propaganda fide*.[2] This has become absolutely imperative at the present day, as is shown by the encyclicals *Maximum illud* of Benedict XV, dated 30 November 1919, *Rerum Ecclesiæ* of Pius XI, dated 18 February 1926, and *Evangelii præcones* of Pius XII, dated 2 June 1951. This last contains not only very definite statements on the need for a native clegy (§§ 23, 25, 26) but also the most explicit pronouncements regarding respect for native civilizations, for the individuality of the different peoples and for all the elements of truth that Christianity may find in them (§§ 58-62).

Immediately after the outbreak of the second world war which Nazi race doctrines had made inevitable, Pope Pius XII took a measure which eloquently conveyed the message the Church has for the world—the message upholding peace and unity above all the barriers that divide race from race and civilization from civilization, while yet recognizing the diversity of humankind; on 29 October 1939, on the Feast of Christ the King, His Holiness consecrated 12 missionary bishops, this new apostolic College including a Chinaman, a French foreign missionary, an Indian Jesuit, a Mexican Salesian, an Italian Dominican, a Dutch Father of the SVD (Steyl), an American, an Irishman, a German Franciscan, a White Father from Belgium, a Madagascan and a Congolese. True catholicity of the Church! The following table gives the figures for the native clergy and foreign missionaries working in mission countries in 1951:[3]

---

[1] Pius V, letter to the King of Portugal, 1571; Urban VII, Bull of 1627.
[2] Instructions of 1630, etc.
[3] Figures given by *Rythmes du Monde,* 1951-52, p. 52.

	Native clergy	Foreign clergy
Africa	1,096	6,366
America	397	1,223
Asia	6,751	5,841
Europe	782	204
Oceania	2,113	2,067
Total	11,139	15,701

It is thus clear that, both in doctrine and in practice, the Church recognizes the facts of "race"; but, so far as the Church is concerned, race is no more a reason for religious discrimination than it is a basis for the imposition of uniformity.

The Church and the Problems involved in the Coexistence of White and Coloured People

The problem to be solved is how life as members of a common society is to be lived by men of different ethnic origins and—more important still—of different and disparate cultural standards. In some countries it is not specially acute. In Brazil, for instance, the practising of any form of racial discrimination by public servants is punishable by law; coloured priests are numerous; and a satisfactory *modus vivendi* has been reached between Indians, Negroes, and whites of Portuguese descent.[1] On the other hand, the question remains a burning one in South Africa, where it is very difficult to solve, and in the United States, where it need not prove so. Only after surveying the position in these two countries will it be possible to grasp the general premises for the Catholic position.

In *South Africa* 8,500,000 Negroes and 300,000 Indians share the country with 2,500,000 whites and 1,000,000 half-castes. The whites are descended from Dutch colonists, French Huguenot refugees or English settlers; 83 per cent of the land and all political power are in their

---

[1] Cf. the Unesco enquiry of 1952, of which the findings are given in *Class and Caste in Rural Brazil* (edited by Charles Wagley) and summarized by Dr. Alfred Métraux in the *Courier*, August-September 1952.

hands. Of the Negroes, no more than five per cent are able to read and write, although a considerable expenditure of effort and money on schools for them has been made. Draconian legislation enforces complete segregation (Apartheid) and prevents any contact, even physical, between white and coloured people; business and industry are run by and for the whites, and the Negroes' part is merely to provide pauper labour, ill-fed, ill-housed and sometimes ill-treated. This state of affairs is the source of social problems, and even scandals and injustices, which books like Alan Paton's novel, *Cry the Beloved Country*, have brought before the bar of world opinion.

In the face of this situation, the Christian churches could not remain silent and indifferent.

On the Protestant side, there have been declarations against racial discrimination, such as that issued by the Christian Council of South Africa in May 1947. On the other hand, the report of the Synodal Commission of the Dutch Reformed Church of South Africa, published in 1951, is susceptible of being read as a justification of Apartheid on Scriptural grounds; but it is not for us here to deal with this view, from which incidentally many pastors, particularly of the younger generation, dissociate themselves.

We must, however, give the substance of the remarkable Pastoral Letter on the social and racial problem issued by the Catholic Archbishop and Bishops of South Africa in May 1952 (see Bibliography). To begin with, the very grave difficulties created by the coexistence of men differing so profoundly in culture and degree of social evolution are acknowledged, and it is conceded that no swift and easy solution can be looked for. Consequently nothing must be done to aggravate the question and to convert the delays in reaching a solution of it into fuel for social and political disorders. The Letter continues, very pertinently: "Were the attitude of Europeans the sole reason for South Africa's racial problem, it would be simple enough to condemn it as unjust and un-Christian, and, by a determined process of education, endeavour to modify it. However, the problem is far more complex than that. Its complexity arises out of the fact that the great majority of non-Europeans, and particularly the Africans, have not yet reached a stage of development that would justify their integration into a homogeneous society with the European. A sudden and violent attempt to force them into the mould of European manners and customs would be disastrous. . . ." There are four things, continues the Letter, that must be dealt with: (a) a deep-rooted prejudice on the part of most Europeans against non-Europeans; (b) on the part of many non-Europeans, resentment and distrust, almost innate in the illiterate, and aggravated in the literate through their experiences and reading to such a degree that they can scarcely conceive that Europeans might want to help them to higher attainments; (c) a group of non-European people in various stages of cultural development, of which the majority is still totally unprepared for full participation in social and political life patterned after what are commonly called Western standards; (d) divisions and animosity between various non-European groups.

The way to an equitable and realistic solution is indicated, under the three heads of *prudence, charity,* and *justice.* Prudence will avoid desperate remedies or spectacular measures that do more harm than good. Charity will supply the driving force and the illumination throughout, always provided that it goes hand in hand with an effective attempt at justice. Justice prescribes recognition of the rights of others, more particularly those rights flowing from the very nature and constitution of man—"the right to life, dignity, sustenance, worship, to the integrity, use and normal development of faculties, to work and the fruit of work, to private ownership of property, to well-being, to sojourn and movement, to marriage and the procreation and education of children, to association with one's fellow-men". Each item of this is matched by a restriction to which non-Europeans in South Africa are daily, in practice, subject. A list is also given of other rights, less fundamental, deriving from man's quality as a social being—"the right to vote in the election of legislative bodies, state aid in education, unemployment insurance, old age pensions, and so on".

The State, it is pointed out, can neither disregard the fundamental rights of man nor limit, arbitrarily, the rights of the citizen; on the contrary, its duty is to create or promote the best conditions for the exercise of those rights. Further, responsibility for carrying out such a policy does not fall to the State alone, it is shared by employers and all those in positions of influence. By way of conclusion, the following list of principles is formulated in the light of the three considerations of charity, justice and prudence:

1. Discrimination based exclusively on grounds of colour is an offence against the right of non-Europeans to their natural dignity as human persons.
2. Though most of the basic rights of non-Europeans are in theory respected, conditions arising out of discriminatory legislation (such as laws restricting employment), social conventions and inefficient administration seriously impair the exercise of these fundamental rights. The disruption of family life is a case in point.
3. Justice demands that non-Europeans be permitted to evolve gradually toward full participation in the political, economic and cultural life of the country.
4. This evolution cannot come about without earnest endeavours on the part of non-Europeans to prepare themselves for the duties connected with the rights they hope to enjoy.

We have made a point of giving the substance of, and extensive quotations from, this remarkable document because it is a concrete example of the attitude and practical policy of the Catholic Church in the face of specific racial situations and problems.

In the *United States* there are some 15,000,000 Negroes, of whom the majority are the descendants of slaves brought from Africa between 1619 and the Civil War of 1861-65. There are also other non-white minorities— Japanese and Puerto Rican—presenting a problem analogous to that of the Negro minority, smaller indeed, but sometimes even more acute; and lastly an Indian minority which, though confined to the Reserves, is of continuing concern to the Federal Government. Only the Negro problem will be considered here. Enough has been written about it to fill several library shelves; and although the Catholic Church has no more than 350,000 Negro adherents, she has not been able to avoid taking a definite theoretical and practical stand.

So far as principle is concerned, the Church's position

is simple. It was enunciated by Mgr. Ireland, Archbishop of St. Paul, on 1 January 1891 in a masterly address delivered on the anniversary of the Act of Emancipation of 1863. After extolling the abolition of slavery, Mgr. Ireland proceeded thus:

"Let us do our full duty. There is work for us. I have said that slavery has been abolished in America; the trail of the serpent, however, yet marks the ground. We do not accord to our black brothers all the rights and privileges of freedom and of a common humanity. They are the victims of an unreasonable and unjustifiable ostracism. They may live, provided they live away from us, as a separate and inferior race, with whom close contact is pollution. It looks as if we had grudgingly granted to them emancipation, as if we fain still would be the masters and hold them in servitude.

"What do I claim for the black man? That which I claim for the white man, neither more nor less. I would blot out the colour line. White men have their estrangements. They separate on lines of wealth, of intelligence, of culture, of ancestry. . . . But let there be no barrier against mere colour.

"Why a barrier of this kind? Where can we find a reason for it? Colour is the merest accident in man, the result of climatic changes. The colours of the human skin are of many different kinds. The shadings of the so-called white race are not easily numbered. Why visit with the ire of our exclusive pride the black, even into its lightest shadings, scarcely discernible to the eye from the olive dark, a shading most admired in the white family of nations?

"Not in race. Men are all of the same race, sprung from the one father and the one mother. Ethnology and the Holy Writ give the same testimony. The sub-divisions of race are but accidental deviations from the parent stock, which revert to the first model as easily with the same length of years as they diverted from it. The notion that God by special interposition marked off the sub-divisions of the human family, and set upon each one an indelible seal of permanence, is the dream of ignorance or bigotry.

"The objection is made that Negroes are of inferior intellectual parts to the whites. I reply, that there are white men inferior on those lines to other white men, and still no wall of separation is built up by the latter against the former. Treat Negroes who are intellectually inferior to us as we treat inferior whites, and I shall not complain. And as to a radical inferiority in the Negro as compared with his white brother, we can afford to deny it in presence of his achievements in the short years which have elapsed since restitution was made to him of his freedom, and any inferiority which exists we may attribute to his unfortunate condition of long centuries whether in America or his native Africa.

"We are the victims of foolish prejudice, and the sooner we free ourselves from it the sooner shall we grow into true manhood. Is it to our honour that we persecute men because of the social conditions of their fathers? It is not so long ago since the proudest peoples of Europe were immersed in barbarism. It is not to our honour that we punish men for the satisfaction of our own pride. Why, the fact that once the Negro was our slave should compel us to treat him with particular liberality, to compensate him if possible for wrong done, and to obliterate in mutual forbearance and favour the sad memories of years gone by.

"I would break down all barriers. Let the Negro be our equal before the law. There are states where the violation in the Negro of the most sacred personal right secured impunity before the law. In many states the law forbids marriage between white and black—in this manner fomenting immorality and putting injury no less upon the white whom it pretends to elevate than upon the black for whose degradation it has no care.

"Let the Negro be our equal in the enjoyment of all political rights of the citizen. The Constitution gives him those rights; let us be loyal to the Constitution. If the education of the Negro does not fit him to be a voter and an office holder, let us, for his sake and our own, hurry to enlighten him.

"I would open to the Negro all industrial and professional avenues—the test for his advance being his ability, but never his colour. I would, in all public gatherings, and in all public resorts, in halls and hotels, treat the black man as I treat the white. I might shun the vulgar man, whatever his colour, but the gentleman, whatever his colour, I would not dare push away from me.

"Shall the homes of the whites be opened to the blacks, shall all meet in the parlour in perfect social equality?

My answer is that one's home is one's castle, the privileged place where one follows out his own likes and his own tastes, and no one, white or black, rich or poor, can pass the door without an invitation from the owner, and no one can pass censure upon the owner's act."

In this splendid text we already find the practical side dealt with in considerable detail; it lays down clear-cut directives. However, in all practical matters there are, between the prescribing of the objectives or directives and the immediate act, certain stages to be traversed, obstacles to be overcome, "psychological moments" to be awaited, and practical limitations to be endured—to say nothing of the resistance put up by selfishness, pride, timidity and worldliness, and the regrettable inertia to which every social entity is liable. "The spirit is willing, but the flesh is weak. . . ."

It is a fact that it is difficult to secure a Negro's admission to hospital: in Pennsylvania for instance, in 1951, only two per cent of beds were allocated to Negroes, though the latter represent 11 per cent of the population. In some states, such as California, the law approves no discrimination, and it often happens that white people are treated by a Negro doctor or dentist. Elsewhere, as in Mississippi and South Carolina, the whites avoid the Negroes to the utmost possible extent. Historical-social complexes are the most enduring of all, and cannot be abolished in a single century; we have only to recall the cases of the Protestants in France and the Catholics in England. The Negroes too have their complexes, which affect the practical terms of the problem; and corresponding complexes are found in the whites, and more particularly—formless but powerful—in white women, among whom an animal fear of the Negro as a potential aggressor is often to be noted. In the American nation the two races share a country, but there is almost no meeting of minds, and as little physical meeting as possible. After the Emancipation, the Second Plenary Council of Baltimore (1866) considered the question whether separate churches should be built for Negroes or whether they should be accepted in the same churches as other believers. It finally left it to each bishop to decide on the alternative which he considered the most salutary.[1] In

---

[1] Article 10, Fourth Decree.

practice, there are very few mixed parishes. The reason is primarily the absence of mixed residential areas: the Negroes have their own districts, and on occasion—even where, as in California, they suffer no discrimination—they come together spontaneously on a basis of origin. However, there are also reasons less comfortable to admit, having their root in colour prejudice pure and simple; and for a Frenchman it is more than mildly shocking to see the faithful divide, according to colour, for the united act of the Eucharist or for a diocesan congress.[1] It is all the pleasanter to be able to point to the Brooklyn parish of the Holy Rosary, which is deliberately inter-racial, or the small Congregationalist parish of Staffordville, where most of the 75 parishioners are whites, but the pastor is a Negro.

For years there was a lack of coloured clergy, even for the needs of the Negroes; only 14 Negro priests were ordained between 1854 and 1934, while as late as 1950 the total number in service was only 33. Today, however, the number of those being called is substantial, and it is anticipated that there will be a thousand coloured priests by 1960. The Holy See is naturally encouraging this trend, and in this connexion we may quote the following lines from the Encyclical *Sertum Lætitiæ* addressed to the Episcopate of the United States by Pius XII on 1 November 1939: "We confess that We feel a special paternal affection, which is certainly inspired of Heaven, for the Negro People dwelling among you; for in the field of religion and education, We know that they need special care and comfort and are very deserving of it. . . ."[2]

Thus American Catholics still have far to travel in a sphere in which their honour as Christians, far more even than their honour as democrats, is involved. The Catholic Inter-Racial Council, an association directed by Father La Farge, S.J., publishes a monthly organ entitled *Inter-Racial Review, A Journal for Christian Democracy*.[3] This takes its stand on the concept of the absolute unity of the Mystical Body and of liturgical

---

[1] Cf. the investigation by Father J. H. Fichter, S.J., *Southern Parish*, Vol. I, University of Chicago Press, 1952.

[2] *Acta Apostolicæ Sedis*, 1939, p. 637; English text, p. 647.

[3] 20 Vesey Street, New York.

worship. It should be added that the clergy are unanimous in sharing these views, while the theological writings available to them are also entirely explicit. Father J. E. Coogon, S.J., writes that discrimination against Negroes in schools and churches is condemned by theologians as "unjust, impious and scandalous".[1] A moralist, J. F. Doherty, writes that there may perhaps be grounds for taking racial differences into account in the case of a proposed marriage. If, however, after due consideration, a person wishes to marry someone of a different race, no law can justly forbid it, and any law doing so would be an unjust law, not binding, therefore, upon the conscience.[2]

To all this evidence, of which an infinity of other examples could easily be found, should be added the full text of the letter sent in March 1952 by Mgr. H. Varin de la Brunelière, Bishop of Fort-de-France (Martinique), to West Indian students resident in France. The bishop goes beyond the mere rejection of race prejudice; he stresses the special qualities of Negroes, and their positive contribution to civilization and to the countries of which they are citizens. The letter glorifies the Negro, but indirectly also glorifies the country of his citizenship: "We have the history of the American Negro to prove the aptitudes of a race. . . . Despite . . . all these obstacles, the Negro population of America has advanced in all fields, and today many Negroes hold enviable positions in the arts, science or industry. It may not be generally known that at the present time American Negroes are running 14 banks, 200 loan societies, 60,000 trading enterprises and 200 insurance companies, that they have about 200 newspapers and periodicals and possess 5,000,000 hectares of land—i.e. an area larger than the Netherlands."[3]

The Church and Nazi Racism and Modern Anti-Semitism

The tradition of the Church is to treat with established régimes, with a view to securing acceptable conditions for the practice of their religion by the faithful and of its ministry by the priesthood. Rome entered into a con-

---

[1] "Christian Untouchables?" in *Review for Religious,* No. 5, 1946, pp. 107-13.

[2] *Moral Problems of Inter-Racial Marriages,* Washington, 1950.

[3] See the full text in *Témoignage Chrétien,* 13 June 1932.

cordat with the Third Reich in July 1933. Her battle, already begun, against Nazi racial doctrines was to become more bitter almost at once, reaching its climax in 1937-38. Unfortunately, this story is all too little known, though it is plainly revealed in reviews and publications of the time. All that can be done in the present study is to recall a few specially significant episodes, not so much of the daily battle waged *on the spot* by thousands of courageous laymen and priests (some of them known to me personally), as of that carried on, likewise on the spot, by the hierarchy and from Rome by the Papacy itself under the Dauntless Christian leadership of Pius XI:

February 1931: Pastoral Letter by the Bavarian Episcopate condemning the errors of racism.

23 January 1933: Pastoral Letter by Mgr. Gfoellner, Bishop of Linz, against paganism and Nazi racism.

December 1933: Sermons by Cardinal Faulhaber condemning the persecution of the Jews.

21 December 1933: Joint Pastoral Letter by the Austrian Episcopate.

9 February 1934: A. Rosenberg's book, *Der Mythus des 20. Jahrhunderts,* placed on the Index.[1]

7 June 1934: Joint Pastoral Letter by the German bishops.

19 June 1935: A. Rosenberg's book, *An die Dunkelmänner unserer Zeit, Eine Antwort auf die Angriffe gegen den "Mythus des 20. Jahrh",* placed on the Index.[2]

14 March 1937: Encyclical by Pius XI, *Mit brennender Sorge,* condemning the doctrines of Nazism;[3] and its reading in the churches consequent upon its clandestine introduction into and distribution in Germany.

19 June 1937: C. Cogni's book *Il Razzismo* placed on the Index.[4]

13 April 1938: Letter from the Sacred Congregation of Seminaries and Universities to Cardinal Baudrillart, charging Catholic scientific establishments to refute the eight propositions summarizing the theses of

---

[1] *Acta Apostolicæ Sedis,* 1934, p. 93.
[2] *Acta Apostolicæ Sedis,* 1935, pp. 304-5.
[3] *Acta Apostolicæ Sedis,* 1937, pp. 145-67.
[4] *Acta Apostolicæ Sedis,* 1937, p. 306.

racism[1] (for the circumstances of publication, see below).

19 April 1938: Joint Pastoral Letter of the German bishops.

3 May 1938: Hitler's visit to Rome. On 30 April, Pius XI left the Vatican for Castel Gandolfo, stating that he could not breathe the air of Rome; he further ordered the closing of the Vatican museums and forbade the decoration of religious establishments with the Nazi colours, saying "Nothing could be less suitable or timely than to fly, on Holy Cross Day, the banner of another cross which is not that of Christ." Furthermore, it was on 3 May that the *Osservatore Romano,* the Vatican newspaper, published the Letter of 13 April against racism, whilst entirely ignoring Hitler's visit to Rome.

15 July 1938: Following the publication, by a group of Fascist scientists, of a document setting out 10 points in favour of racism and anti-Semitism, address by Pius XI against "exaggerated nationalism which raises barriers between the peoples".[2]

21 July 1938: Address by Pius XI condemning exaggerated nationalism and racism, and affirming the world-wide unity of the Church.[3]

21 July 1938: Address by Pius XI to the students of the College of Propaganda, representing 37 different nations: "The word Catholic means universal. . . . We would have none cut off from the human family. . . . The term *human genus* reveals the unity of the human race . . . , though it cannot be denied that within that universal race there is room for racial as for so many other kinds of variation. . . . We may well ask our-

---

[1] The first six of these propositions are as follows: (a) The races of mankind, by their natural and immutable characteristics, differ so widely that the lowest among them is further from the highest than from the highest animal species. (b) It is necessary to use all means to preserve and cultivate the vigour of the race and the purity of the blood; everything conducing to this end is, on that ground alone, right and permissible. (c) The blood, the seat of the race's characteristics, is the principal source from which all the intellectual and moral qualities of man derive. (d) The essential aim of education is to develop the characteristics of the race and to kindle in men's minds a burning love of their own race as the supreme good. (e) Religion is subordinate to the law of race and must be adjusted to it. (f) The primary source and supreme rule of the whole legal order is racial instinct.

[2] *Osservatore Romano,* 17 July.

[3] *Osservatore Romano,* 23 July.

52

selves how it comes about that Italy should unhappily have needed to imitate Germany. . . . He who eats Pope dies of it. . . . Human dignity consists in the fact that we are a single great family, the human genus, the human race. . . . That is the Church's answer, that, in the Church's eyes, is the true racism. . . ."[1]

6 November 1938: Address by Cardinal Faulhaber, Archbishop of Munich, on the Christian sense of fellowship through faith and not through blood.

November 1938: Publication by Cardinal van Roey, Archbishop of Malines, of an address condemning racism and its "blood myth".

17 November 1938: Letter from Cardinal Verdier, Archbishop of Paris, associating himself with Mgr. van Roey's statement.

13 November 1938: Address by Cardinal Schuster, Archbishop of Milan, taking issue with the racial myth.

6 January 1939: Address by Cardinal Piazza, Patriarch of Venice, condemning racist anti-Semitism and justifying the Church's attitude to the Jews.[2]

It is impossible, in this study, to deal with a question so complex as that of anti-Semitism and the Catholic Church's position with regard to the "Jewish question". Moreover, there is an abundance of good books on the subject (see Bibliography). Certain conclusions emerge fairly clearly from the most recent acts and publications, and more particularly from the Pastoral Letters of Mgr. Gfoellner (23 January 1933) and the Austrian bishops (21 December 1933), from Cardinal Faulhaber's sermons, from Cardinal Piazza's address (6 January 1939) and from the various protests by the French bishops against the treatment of the Jews in France after July 1942.[3] As regards religion and respect for the human person and the primary natural rights, the Catholic protest against anti-Semitism is definite, united and absolute;[4] it is equally so in the matter of anti-

[1] *Osservatore Romano*, 23 July.

[2] *Osservatore Romano*, 19 January.

[3] See the actual texts in *Documentation catholique*, 42, 1945, columns 87 et seq. and 119 et seq.; E. Guerry, *L'Eglise catholique en France sous l'Occupation*, Paris, 1947, p. 33 et seq.

[4] The decree of the Holy Office of 25 March 1928 is apposite: "because it reproves all hatred and all animosity between the peoples, it [the Holy See] condemns, unreservedly, hatred of the people once chosen by God, that hatred which is today commonly called anti-semitism" (*Acta Apostolicæ Sedis*, 1928, p. 104.

Jewish discrimination based on racism. As regards the political and sociological aspects of the question, the Catholic attitude is qualified. For example, in pre-1939 Hungary the Catholic bishops, as members of Parliament, accepted the *numerus clausus* laid down for the admission of Jews to certain professions and schools. Here the bishops were acting as national leaders in a country where the Jewish minority (5.3 per cent of the population) had a practical monopoly in a number of spheres (press, theatre, etc.) or at the least had a higher proportion of posts than its numbers warranted, even taking its cultural level into account. This is only one example among many of the kind of social or political questions that may arise. The pronouncements by the pastoral Magisterium, already quoted, recognize that such questions exist; with the assertion that they cannot be resolved without the fullest regard for the dictates of justice, human dignity and even charity, there goes, nevertheless, implicit recognition that there are certain practical problems which consideration of the fact of Jewry from a purely religious or mystical angle neither abolishes nor solves. Even those Catholic thinkers who, like Jacques Maritain, are primarily concerned with Israel as a supernatural mystery, and proclaim that anti-Semitism of any kind strikes at the heart of it, do not omit brief consideration at least of the practical problems raised by a certain particularism and a restless, enterprising attitude characteristic of the Jews. Despite the plainest and sincerest declarations against religious, philosophical or racist anti-Semitism, there is in truth a Jewish problem; it is raised by the Jews themselves, from whose minds and thoughts it is, fundamentally, never absent.

However, recent events and Israel's unbelievable sufferings have given us a clearer idea of the harmfulness of anti-Semitism and the virtual impossibility of reaching a *true and just* solution even of concrete political and sociological questions if we permit the leaven of anti-Semitism to work in us. In principle, the *numerus clausus*, which is sometimes introduced in various parts of the world for other ethnic minorities, should not be unjust. In practice, it is in itself a form of racial discrimination; it grows, by a series of imperceptible but logical accretions, into the persecutions condemned by every man worthy of the name. We have here a microbe which does not infect the whole organism from the very beginning but is, even at that stage, infectious and harmful. It must be extirpated wholly. The practical problems, if any, presented by the social fact of Judaism must be approached with the mind, heart and imagination purged of every trace of anti-Semitism, i.e. of the slightest tendency to assent to discrimination against any man on the mere ground of his being a Jew.

Furthermore, from the merely sociological standpoint of the welfare of the community it is sought to protect, anti-Semitism is equally unhealthy. Not only does it serve to replace a diagnosis of the real ills and thus amount, politically, to a loss of direction, but it is corrupt in itself and thus corrupts even what it seeks to serve. "It is allegedly in the name of the common weal that anti-Semitism is fomented; the end result, however, is the corruption and brutalization of those incited to it, through the elevation in them of those instincts which are the lowest, the most immoral, and the most incompatible with human social life."[1] The concrete problems which the fact of Judaism raises must be resolved by each type of man along lines that do not betray his ideal—by the Christian in conformity with his philosophy and his *mystique,* and by "political" or "economic man" through activity stimulated by that of the Jews (whose role it is to provide a ferment) and through legislation that will effectively counter the dissolvent factors, in which the Jews have certainly no monopoly.

---

[1] Y. de Montcheuil, Dec. 1940.

CONCLUSION

One conclusion is to be drawn from the Church's attitude towards the three great concrete problems which we have just reviewed. In every case we have seen that the Church rejects the principles of racism in their entirety but does give weight to the facts of race and to the concrete historical circumstances in which racial problems are moving towards a valid solution. The Church thus combines healthy realism and untainted idealism. But its realism is informed throughout by its ideals, and its idealism is realistic. The two are like two facets of the same truth and here, as everywhere, the truth makes men free. It could easily be shown that there is no better barrier to racism and racial discrimination than a healthy and realistic recognition of the facts of race and of historical or cultural inequalities. The well known Swedish enquirer, Gunnar Myrdal, has found grounds for the view[1] that racial differences are a factor to be taken into account by democratic countries professing the ideal of equality and seeking to justify their inability to attain that ideal. Here again, healthy realism regarding the facts is the best guarantee of a genuine ideal of equality.

The Church is not racist, indeed she is the antithesis of racism; she stands for the unity of the human family, yet for a unity which does not exclude diversities but rather comprehends them, because it is "catholic". However, the Church recognizes that in the temporal sphere the coexistence of different human groups within a single society does present difficult problems, not because of any radical inequality *per se* between the races which such groups actually or allegedly represent, but because the groups as constituted are at different cultural and political and hence at different "human" levels—for this

---

[1] *An American Dilemma*, New York, 1944.

adjective is not merely a biological description, but has positive cultural connotations. Even in places where, as is usually the case in France, the condition of fellowship in the community is one's way of feeling and living and not race or colour, it is obvious that an excessive difference in levels of human evolution would prevent assimilation and, if a whole group was involved, would present a serious problem. What would Frenchmen do if, as in South Africa, they were living side by side with a whole Kaffir nation?

It is essential to be absolutely clear on this point. The inequalities are real human inequalities; but they have nothing to do with any hereditary or genetically inevitable inferiority. They spring from the chances of history and sometimes of geography. What time causes time can also change. The Norwegians were a backward people when Byzantium represented the greatest civilization of the world; at various points in history the Egyptians were the teachers of Greece, and the Arabs of the West; and the Chinese, before their culture became static and thus acted as a brake on them, were several centuries ahead of Europe. It may be that the future belongs to peoples who today are outside the main stream of history. Let us then by all means talk of factual inequalities of a cultural, social or political nature, but not of essential inequalities dependent on genetic factors.

From this flow consequences of the utmost importance. Firstly, inequalities in development do not involve any essential inequalities. Secondly, essential equality does not necessarily imply actual equality in every respect in the sphere of cultural, social and political life. The overriding principle of human unity must indeed invariably be deferred to, but it does not do away with cultural gradations. All men are equal in essence, and this is reflected in their equality in natural primary rights, those comprehended in the term "dignity of the human person". But there are men who cannot read or do not wash, and others who do wash and do read. The latter are under no obligation to associate with the former for all purposes at all costs; they are however bound, by the brotherly duty created by the unity of the human family, to help them to educate themselves, and to learn to read and wash.

Such, we think, are the general ideas determining the

Church's attitude in practice. The Church herself sets human societies an example of good faith. She proclaims *and applies* the principle of the unity and equality of all men. She helps forward the less advanced, and even commits authority to them as soon as they are in a position to assume it. The Church *is* unity; but within that unity there is an extraordinary diversity, and to that diversity, which includes the diversity of races (in so far as there are races), she gives a positive and sanctified meaning.

GENERAL

Acta Apostolicæ Sedis. Rome, Vatican Press (official organ of the Holy See).

CHARLES, P., FOLLIET, J., LORSON, P., VAN CAMPENHOUT, E. *Racisme et catholicisme.* Paris and Tournai, Casterman, 1939 (separate printing of the February 1939 number of the *Nouvelle revue théologique*).

Documentation catholique. Paris, Bonne Presse.

Hérédités et races. Juvisy, Edit. du Cerf, 1931.

Religion des Blutes . . . Sonderheft der Zeitschrift "Eine Heilige Kirche". Ed. by Fr. Heiler, Munich, Reinhardt, July-September 1936.

SCHRÖDER, Chr.-M. *Rasse und Religion.* Munich, Reinhardt, 1937.

STERILIZATION

JORDAN, Ed., VIOLLET, J., TIBERGHIEN, P. *Eugénisme, stérilisation. Leur valeur morale.* Paris, Association du mariage chrétien.

MARTIN DE SOBRADILLO, Agapito. *La procréation et la stérilisation du point de vue du droit naturel.* Fribourg, (Switzerland) 1932.

MUCKERMANN, H. *Eugenik und Katholizismus.* Berlin, 1934.

MISSIONS AND RACES

BERG. "Mission und Rassenversöhnung", *Die katholische Heidenmission als Kulturträger.* 10 vols., 1925.

BOURGEOIS, Ch. "L'appel des races au catholicisme", *Xaveriana.* Louvain, 10th series, nos. 109 and 118, January and October 1933.

BUHLMANN, W. *Die christliche Terminologie als missions-methodisches Problem* . . . Schöneck-Beckentied, Switzerland, 1950.

Der einheimische Klerus in Geschichte und Gegenwart. Homage to Laurenz Kilger. Schöneck-Beckentied, Switzerland, 1950.

KILGER, L. "Rasse und Nation in der neueren Missionszeit", *Kathol. Missionsjahrbuch der Schweiz.* 1939, pp. 84-98.

LEHMACHER. "Rasse und Glaubensverbreitung", *Die katholischen Missionen.* 1934, pp. 12 ff., 39 ff., 70 ff.

ROWLEY, H. H. *The Missionary Message of the Old Testament.* London, 1945.

THAUREN, J. "Mission und Rassenversöhnung", *Pensiero Missionario.* 1931, pp. 17ff.

SOUTH AFRICA

"Pastoral Letter of the Archbishops and Bishops of South Africa, met at Mariannhill (Natal), May 1952", published in *The Sword*, No. 160 (September-October 1952), pp. 12 ff.; reproduced by the News Service of the National Catholic Welfare Conference (New York), 27 June 1952; French translation in *Documentation catholique*, 19 October 1952, columns 1326-30; summary and extracts in German in *Herder-Korrespondenz*, 6 (1952), pp. 510-12. This statement by the South African Episcopate was supplemented, in September 1952, by a statement by Mgr. Hurley, Archbishop of Durban, to the South African Institute on Race Relations (cf. *Herder-Korrespondenz*, November 1952, pp. 64 ff.).

Race Relations Journal. A quarterly journal published by the South African Institute of Race Relations. Johannesburg.

Race Relations News. Published monthly by the South African Institute of Race Relations. Johannesburg.

The South African Outlook. A Journal dealing with Missionary and Racial Affairs. Lovedale (primarily concerned with educational questions; non-Catholic).

Tydskrif vir Tasse-Aangeleenthede. Journal of Racial Affairs. Sabra.

UNITED STATES OF AMERICA

CANTWELL, Daniel M. *Catholics speak on Race Relations.*
GILLARD, T. J., S.J. *Coloured Catholics in the United States.*
GILLIGAN, F. J. *The Morality of the Colour Line.* Washington, The Catholic University Press, 1928.
TWOMEY, L. J., S.J. *How to think about Race?* St. Louis, 1951.

THE CHURCH AGAINST NAZI RACISM

NEUHAUSLER, J. *Kreuz und Hakenkreuz. Der Kampf des Nationalsozialismus gegen die katholische Kirche und der kirchliche Widerstand.* 2 vols., Munich, Verlag der Kathol. Kirch Bayerns, 1946.
SOLZBACHER, W. *Pius XI als Verteidiger der menschlichen Persönlichkeit.* Lucerne, 1939, pp. 91-179.
The French works by K. Türmer and R. d'Harcourt.
The various official documents quoted have appeared, in the case of those issued from Rome, either in the *Acta Apostolicæ Sedis* or in the *Osservatore Romano,* and in the case of the remainder, in French translation or summary in *Documentation catholique.* The quoted statements by Cardinals van Roey, Verdier, Schuster and Cerejeira have been collected in a booklet entitled *L'Eglise contre le racisme: une hérésie anti-romaine.* Paris, Bonne Presse, 1938.

THE JEWISH QUESTION AND ANTI-SEMITISM

CLAUDEL, P., and others. *Les Juifs.* Paris, Plon, 1937.
"Die Kirche Christi und die Judenfrage", articles by a number of Catholic scholars published in the review *Die Erfüllung.* Vienna, 1937.
FÉRENZY, O. DE. *Les Juifs et nous, chrétiens.* Paris, 1935.
JOURNET, Ch. *Destinées d'Israël. A propos du salut par les Juifs.* Paris, Egloff, 1947.
"Les Juifs et nous", *Chronique sociale de France.* Lyon, 1952, No. 1.
MARITAIN, J. *L'impossible antisémitisme.* Paris, Desclée, 1938.

MONTCHEUIL, Y. DE. "Le chrétien en face de l'antisémitisme", lecture given in December 1940 and published in *L'Eglise et le monde actuel*. Paris, Témoignage chrétien, 1945, pp. 101-17.

PETERSON, E. *Die Kirche aus Juden und Heiden*. Salzburg, Kösel, 1933 (French translation, *Le mystère des Juifs et des Gentils dans l'Eglise*. Paris, Desclée).

[A.133] $0.50; 2/6 (stg.); 1.75 F